Write your name.

Z z

Bees are very busy creatures. They go from flower to flower collecting pollen and buzzing busily, ZZZZZZZZZ.

Action: Put arms out at sides and pretend to be a bee, saying ZZZZZZZZZ.

buzzing bee

buzzing bee

Z Capital

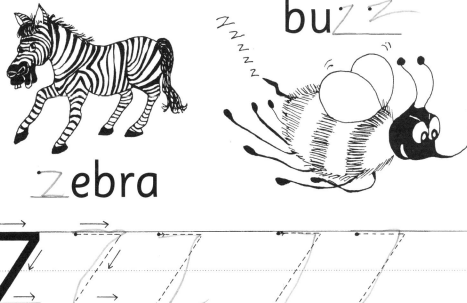

zebra

bu zz

Z

One day the wind and the sun had a competition. "I will blow that man's coat off", said the wind, *wh, wh, wh.*
The man held on to his coat.
The sun shone, brighter and hotter, until the man took off his coat.

W w

Action: Blow onto open hand, as if you are the wind, and say *wh, wh, wh.*

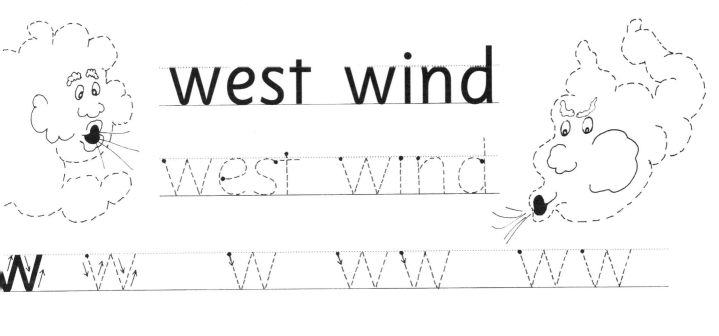

west wind

west wind

W w w w ww ww
w w w ww ww

The letter ‹w› goes diagonally down to the line.

WW www www

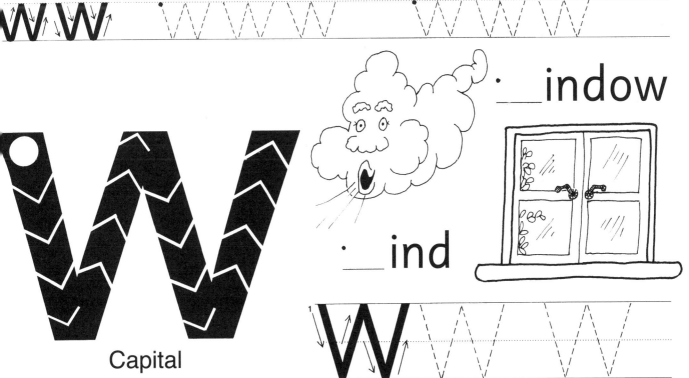

Capital

__indow

__ind

W

ng

Inky pretends she is a weightlifter. She lifts the broom up saying *ng*...

Action: Imagine you are a weightlifter and pretend to lift a heavy weight above your head saying *ng* ...

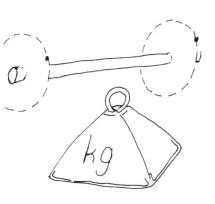

strong

strong

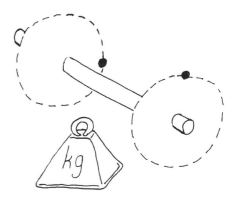

ng

ng ng ng ng

ng ng ng ng ng

ng ng ng ng

ri___

ka___aroo

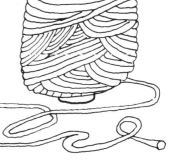

stri___

7

Uncle Vic drives a van. He drives
from place to place, *vvvvvvvv.*

V v

Action: Pretend to be holding the steering wheel of a van
and say *vvvvvvvv.*

Vic's van

Vic's van

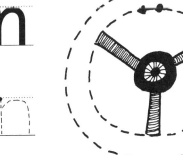

V

V V

The letter ‹v› goes diagonally down to the line, like a ‹w›.

V V

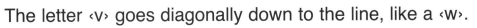

Capital

V

·_iolin

·_an

ca_e

V

9

To show the different sounds, the oo (as in foot) and oo (as in moon) are shown with thin and fat letters.

Short oo

Long oo

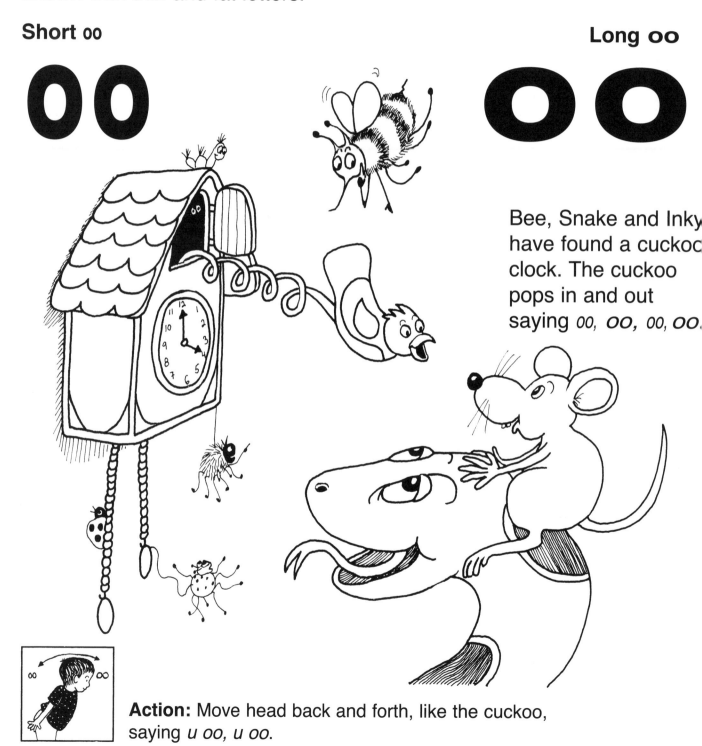

Bee, Snake and Inky have found a cuckoo clock. The cuckoo pops in and out saying *oo, oo, oo, oo.*

Action: Move head back and forth, like the cuckoo, saying *u oo, u oo.*

cuckoo clock

cuckoo clock

n writing, an ordinary ‹oo› is used.

oo

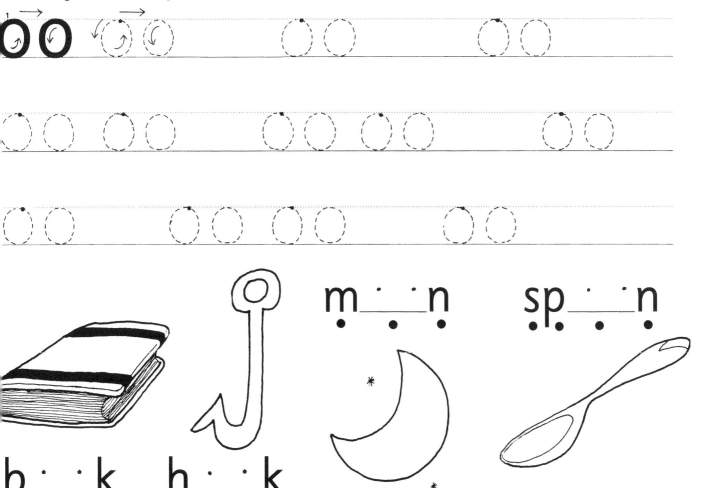

b _ _ k   h _ _ k   m _ _ n   sp _ _ n

When reading, try the /oo/ sound first. If this does not make a word, try using the /oo/ sound.

Alphabet

Put the little letters next to the capitals.

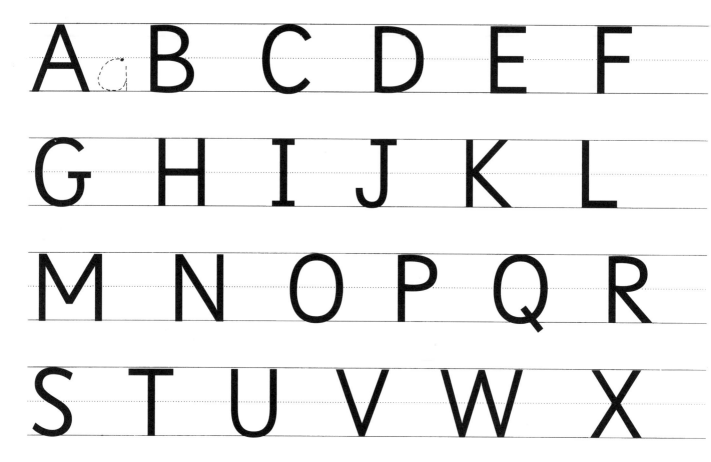

A a B C D E F

G H I J K L

M N O P Q R

S T U V W X

Write *your* initials here:

Y Z

Put these groups of words into alphabetical order.

sun	fun	run	bun
bun	___	___	___

pig	hen	dog	cat
___	___	___	___

Bee	Snake	Ant	Inky
___	___	___	___

The alphabet has been divided into four groups. Learning the groups will help you tell which quarter of the dictionary any letter will be in.

Complete the groups.

1. A _ _ D _

2. F _ H _ _ K _ M

3. _ O _ _ R _

4. T _ V _ X _ _

Choose a letter. Which quarter is it in?
Can you open the dictionary at that letter?

Write each word.

—— —— ——

—— —— ——

—— —— —— ——   —— —— ——   —— —— ——

Magic

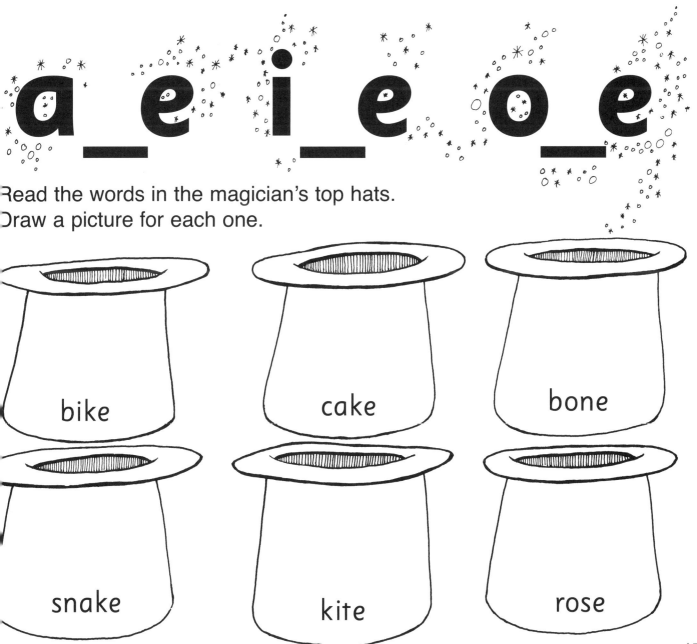

The magic e changes the previous vowel from its sound to its name.

a_e   i_e   o_e

Read the words in the magician's top hats.
Draw a picture for each one.

bike

cake

bone

snake

kite

rose

15

Join each word to its picture.

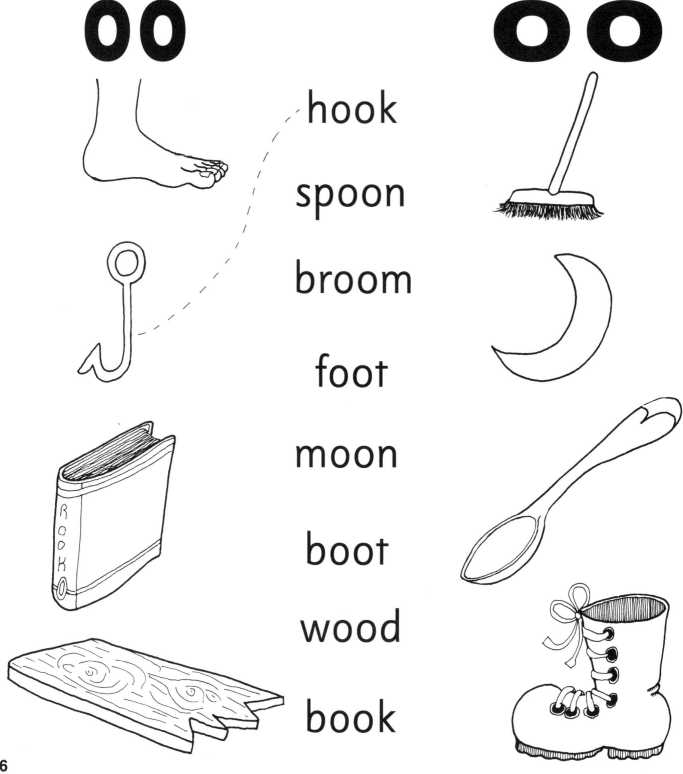

hook

spoon

broom

foot

moon

boot

wood

book

Help the spiders spin their webs.

Join each sentence to its picture.

A duck on a pond.

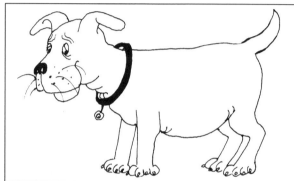

A cat and 3 kittens.

A rabbit and a carrot.

A big fat dog.

Mnemonics is another way of learning to spell tricky words.

laugh

laugh **at ug**ly **g**oat's **h**air

people

people **e**at **o**melettes **p**eople **l**ike **e**ggs

Say each picture, and choose the correct way to write /ie/.

ie   i_e   y   igh

__ __ c _   k __ __ __   __ __ __ __

___   c __ __   __ __ __

__ __ __   __ __ __   _ k _

Long Letters and Tall Letters

Practice forming the long letters and the tall letters.
Trace over the dotted letters and words.

Say each picture, and choose the correct way to write /ai/.

ai   a_e   ay

— — — —   — — — —   — — — —

— — — —   — — — —   — — — —

— — — —   wh— — — —   — — —

Numbers need to be formed correctly too.
Workbook 5 - Number 5)

1 2 3 4 5

Count the butterflies.

5 5 5 5 5 5 5 5

Find the five butterflies.

five five five five

Activity

oo oo clock

Make your own oo oo clock.

Draw your clock on a piece of card.
Write oo and oo.
Make a cuckoo but make sure he has a long piece of card.

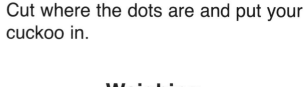

Cut where the dots are and put your cuckoo in.

Bees

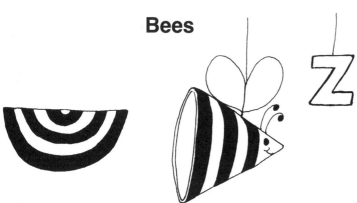

Flying bee z z z z

Cut out a semi circle of card.
Give it yellow and black stripes.
Fix the 2 sides together to form a cone.
Cut some wings from tissue paper.
Give your bee some eyes.

Weighing
See how strong you are.

Do some weighing.

Can you find something that weighs less than you, or more than you?